CHRISTINE HAGGINS

Prayers for Healing and Well-being

Finding Comfort, Renewing Strength, and Experiencing Wholeness

Copyright © 2023 by Christine Haggins

All rights reserved. No part of this publication may be reproduced, stored or transmitted in any form or by any means, electronic, mechanical, photocopying, recording, scanning, or otherwise without written permission from the publisher. It is illegal to copy this book, post it to a website, or distribute it by any other means without permission.

First edition

This book was professionally typeset on Reedsy. Find out more at reedsy.com

Contents

INTRODUCTION	vi
COMPANION GUIDE	x
CHAPTER 1: PRAYERS FOR PHYSICAL HEALING	1
Prayer for Divine Restoration and Healing	1
Prayer for Strength and Recovery	3
Prayer for Pain Relief and Comfort	4
CHAPTER 2: PRAYERS FOR EMOTIONAL HEALING	8
Prayer for Inner Healing and Renewal	8
Prayer for Release from Anxiety and Fear	10
Prayer for Healing from Past Trauma	13
CHAPTER 3: PRAYERS FOR MENTAL HEALTH	17
Prayer for Clarity and Peace of Mind	17
Prayer for Overcoming Depression and Grief	18
Prayer for Healing from Mental Struggles	20

CHAPTER 4: PRAYERS FOR SPIRITUAL HEALING 23
  Prayer for Spiritual Renewal and Refreshing 23
  Prayer for Inner Peace and Serenity 24
  Prayer for Restoring Faith and Hope 26

CHAPTER 5: PRAYERS FOR RELATIONAL HEALING 28
  Prayer for Reconciliation in Relationships 28
  Prayer for Forgiveness and Letting Go 30
  Prayer for Restoring Broken Bonds 31

CHAPTER 6: PRAYERS FOR HEALING IN TIMES OF LOSS 34
  Prayer for Comfort in Grief and Loss 34
  Prayer for Healing from the Pain of Bereavement 36
  Prayer for Strength and Hope in Times of Mourning 37

CHAPTER 7: PRAYERS FOR HEALING IN MARRIAGE AND FAMILY 40
  Prayer for Restoring Love and Unity in Marriage 40
  Prayer for Healing and Reconciliation in Family 43
  Prayer for Blessings and Restoration in Parent-Child Relationships 46

CHAPTER 8: PRAYERS FOR INNER STRENGTH AND EMPOWERMENT	50
Prayer for Courage and Confidence	50
Prayer for Overcoming Challenges and Obstacles	51
Prayer for Empowerment and Steadfastness	51
CHAPTER 9: PRAYERS FOR OVERALL WELL-BEING	53
Prayer for a Healthy Mind, Body, and Spirit	53
Prayer for Emotional Balance and Stability	54
Prayer for Gratitude and Contentment	54
CONCLUSION	56

INTRODUCTION

In the midst of life's challenges, we often find ourselves in need of healing, whether it be physical, emotional, mental, or spiritual. This book is a compilation of heartfelt prayers that seek to bring comfort, renewal, and wholeness to those who are seeking healing in various aspects of their lives.

Within these pages, you will discover a collection of prayers that address different dimensions of healing and well-being. Each prayer is crafted with love, empathy, and a deep understanding of the struggles we face as human beings. They are designed to provide solace in times of pain, guidance in moments of confusion, and strength when we feel weak.

Chapter 1 focuses on prayers for physical healing. Whether you are facing illness, injury, or chronic pain, these prayers seek to invoke divine restoration and offer comfort during times of physical struggle. They are an invitation to trust in God's healing power and experience the renewal of strength and vitality.

Chapter 2 delves into prayers for emotional healing. We all encounter emotional wounds and scars along life's journey. These prayers are a source of support and encouragement as we seek inner healing, release from anxiety and fear, and freedom from past trauma. They remind us that emotional well-being is an essential part of our overall health and happiness.

In Chapter 3, we explore prayers for mental health. In a world that can be overwhelming and demanding, it is crucial to take care of our minds and seek healing from mental struggles such as depression, grief, and anxiety. These prayers offer solace, clarity, and peace of mind as we navigate the complexities of our thoughts and emotions.

Chapter 4 focuses on prayers for spiritual healing. Our spiritual well-being is deeply connected to our overall sense of wholeness. These prayers provide a pathway for inner renewal, restoring our faith, and finding serenity in our relationship with the divine. They guide us towards a deeper connection with our spiritual selves and offer a source of strength during times of spiritual dryness.

In Chapter 5, we address prayers for relational healing. Relationships can be a source of both joy and pain. These prayers are intended to facilitate reconciliation, forgiveness, and the restoration of broken bonds. Whether it is healing a broken friendship, mending a strained family relationship, or finding peace in a challenging marriage, these prayers offer hope and guidance.

Chapter 6 offers prayers for healing in times of loss. Grief can be an overwhelming experience, and these prayers provide comfort, strength, and hope to those who are navigating the journey of mourning. They serve as a reminder that healing is possible even in the midst of profound loss, and that our loved ones will always hold a special place in our hearts.

Chapter 7 centers around prayers for healing in marriage and family. The dynamics within our closest relationships can sometimes become strained and in need of healing. These prayers focus on restoring love, unity, and blessings in marriages, and seek reconciliation and wholeness in family connections.

Chapter 8 addresses prayers for inner strength and empowerment. Life presents us with challenges, obstacles, and moments of self-doubt. These prayers are meant to ignite courage, confidence, and resilience within us. They remind us that we are never alone, and that we have the power to overcome and thrive.

Lastly, Chapter 9 offers prayers for overall well-being. These prayers encompass our holistic health, recognizing the interconnectedness of our mind, body, and spirit. They encourage gratitude, contentment, and a sense of balance in our lives.

As you embark on this journey of healing and well-being through prayer, may these words provide you with comfort, guidance, and renewed hope.

COMPANION GUIDE

As you journey through the different prayers in this book, you might want to keep a journal close to pen down revelations and personal request.

This Prayer Request Journal specifically made for this purpose is all you need.

valleys of recovery. As we face setbacks and obstacles, remind us of Your faithfulness and the promise of healing that lies ahead.

Lord, we surrender our bodies to Your healing touch, recognizing that You are the ultimate healer. May Your grace flow through us, bringing restoration to every part of our being. Give us the patience to trust in Your timing, knowing that Your plans are perfect and that You work all things together for our good.

We offer this prayer in faith, believing that You are able to do immeasurably more than we can ask or imagine. May Your healing power be manifested in our lives, bringing glory to Your name.

In Your loving embrace, we find strength.

Amen.

Prayer for Pain Relief and Comfort

Gracious Lord,

We come before You with hearts burdened by pain and discomfort. In this moment of prayer, we seek relief and comfort from the physical anguish that we bear. We ask for Your healing touch to alleviate our pain and bring us comfort in the midst of our suffering.

Lord, You understand our pain intimately, for You bore our afflictions on the cross. You are our Divine Comforter, who promises to be near to the brokenhearted and to bind up their wounds. We lay our pain before You, trusting in Your compassionate love and mercy.

As we endure physical suffering, grant us relief from the intensity of our pain. Ease our discomfort and grant us moments of respite. Pour out Your healing balm upon our bodies, soothing our nerves, relaxing our muscles, and calming our inflamed or injured tissues. Bring us the comfort that surpasses understanding, filling us with a deep sense of peace even in the midst of physical distress.

Lord, we acknowledge that pain can be not only physical but also emotional and spiritual. Heal not only our bodies but also the inner wounds that contribute to our suffering. Bring healing to the places where our bodies and souls intersect, restoring harmony and balance to our entire being.

In moments when pain feels overwhelming, grant us

the work You have begun in us.

As we receive Your healing, Lord, may we also become vessels of healing for others. Teach us to extend compassion, understanding, and support to those who are walking their own healing journeys. Use our stories of overcoming trauma to offer hope and encouragement to those who are still in the midst of their pain.

In Your presence, O God, we find refuge and strength. You are the Divine Physician who brings restoration to our brokenness. We surrender our past hurts and traumas to You, trusting that You are able to make all things new.

May this prayer be a catalyst for healing in our lives and in the lives of others. May Your grace abound, and may Your healing power flow through us, bringing wholeness and well-being to all who seek Your touch.

In the name of Jesus, our ultimate Healer, we pray.

Amen.

CHAPTER 3: PRAYERS FOR MENTAL HEALTH

Prayer for Clarity and Peace of Mind

Gracious God,

In the midst of the noise and busyness of life, we come before You seeking clarity and peace of mind. Our thoughts can become tangled, overwhelmed by worries, doubts, and distractions. But in Your presence, we find stillness and the reassurance that You hold all things together.

Grant us a calm and focused mind, O Lord. Clear away the clutter and confusion that cloud our thoughts. Help us to let go of anxiety and restlessness, and instead, anchor our minds in Your truth and promises. Fill our minds with thoughts that are pure, true, noble, and praiseworthy.

As we seek clarity, we ask for Your guidance and wisdom. Illuminate the paths before us, helping us to discern Your will and the steps we need to take. Teach us to align our thoughts with Your truth, to view ourselves and the world through the lens of Your love and grace.

Lord, we also pray for those who struggle with mental health challenges. We lift them up to Your loving care, knowing that You are the Great Healer of body, mind, and spirit. Bring comfort to those who are burdened by anxiety, depression, or other mental struggles. Pour out Your peace that surpasses all understanding, guarding their hearts and minds in Christ Jesus.

Prayer for Overcoming Depression and Grief

Compassionate God,

In moments of deep sadness and grief, we turn to You for solace and strength. We lift up those who are weighed down by the heavy burden of depression and grief, knowing that You are near to the brokenhearted and that You offer comfort to those who mourn.

Lord, we ask for Your healing touch upon the minds and hearts of those who battle depression. Bring light into the darkness, replacing despair with hope and joy. Renew their strength and restore their sense of purpose. Surround them with Your love and the support of caring individuals who can walk alongside them on their journey toward healing.

We also lift up those who are grieving the loss of loved ones. Comfort them in their sorrow, Lord, and grant them the space to mourn and process their emotions. Bring them the assurance of Your presence and the hope of eternal life in Christ Jesus. Help them to find healthy ways to honor the memory of their loved ones and to navigate the challenges that come with grief.

Lord, we know that the journey toward healing from depression and grief can be long and arduous. But we trust in Your faithfulness and in the promise that You are close to the brokenhearted. Strengthen our faith and help us to support one another with compassion and understanding.

Prayer for Healing from Mental Struggles

Healing God,

We come before You, acknowledging that mental struggles can be just as challenging as physical ailments. We lift up to You those who battle with anxiety, OCD, addiction, trauma-related disorders, or any other form of mental distress. We ask for Your healing touch upon their minds and spirits, knowing that You are able to bring restoration and wholeness.

Lord, we pray for Your divine intervention in the lives of those who feel trapped by their mental struggles. Break the chains that bind them, release them from the grip of fear and torment, and bring them freedom and liberation. Restore their minds to a state of balance, peace, and well-being.

In Your mercy, provide them with the necessary support and resources they need for their journey toward healing. Surround them with a network of understanding and compassionate individuals who can offer guidance, counseling, and practical assistance. Grant them the courage to seek help and to engage in the healing process.

Lord, we also pray for a greater understanding and

compassion within our communities toward those who struggle with mental struggles. Help us to break down the stigma and misunderstandings surrounding mental health, so that all individuals can find the support and acceptance they deserve.

Grant us, O Lord, the wisdom and discernment to recognize when someone is in need of help. Give us the words to offer encouragement, the ears to listen without judgment, and the hearts to extend compassion. Teach us to be a source of comfort and understanding for those who are hurting.

As we pray for healing from mental struggles, we also acknowledge the importance of holistic well-being. Help us to prioritize self-care and to create a healthy balance in our lives. Guide us in making choices that promote mental, emotional, and spiritual well-being. Show us the importance of seeking professional help when needed, and grant us the courage to take those steps.

Lord, we know that true healing comes from You. You are the Divine Physician who understands the intricate workings of our minds and the depths of our hearts. Pour out Your grace upon all those who are in need of mental healing, and restore them to a place of wholeness and peace.

May this chapter serve as a reminder that no struggle is too great for Your healing touch. May it inspire us to be advocates for mental health, fostering an environment of love, understanding, and acceptance. May it bring hope to those who feel trapped in their mental struggles, assuring them that there is light at the end of the tunnel.

In Your name, O God, we pray for healing and well-being. Amen.

CHAPTER 4: PRAYERS FOR SPIRITUAL HEALING

Prayer for Spiritual Renewal and Refreshing

Heavenly Father,

In the depths of our souls, we long for spiritual renewal and refreshing. We yearn to draw closer to You, to experience Your presence in a profound and transformative way. We confess that at times our spirits grow weary and our hearts become distant. But we know that in You, there is abundant grace and the promise of renewal.

Pour out Your Holy Spirit upon us, O Lord. Revive our spirits, awakening within us a hunger for Your truth and a thirst for Your righteousness. Breathe new life into our weary souls, infusing us with Your love and power. Help us to shed the burdens that weigh us down, releasing them into Your capable hands.

As we seek spiritual renewal, guide us in deepening our relationship with You. Open our eyes to behold the wonders of Your creation, reminding us of Your majesty and sovereignty. Illuminate Your Word, that it may be a lamp to our feet and a light to our path. Stir within us a passion for prayer, that we may commune with You intimately and find solace in Your presence.

Lord, we acknowledge that spiritual renewal is a process that requires surrender and discipline. We lay down our pride, our self-sufficiency, and our distractions. Help us to prioritize time spent with You, cultivating a vibrant and flourishing spiritual life. Grant us the wisdom to discern the things that hinder our spiritual growth and empower us to make the necessary changes.

Prayer for Inner Peace and Serenity

Prince of Peace,

In a world filled with turmoil and unrest, we seek Your gift of inner peace and serenity. Our hearts long for tranquility amidst the chaos, for a calm that surpasses understanding. We bring before You our anxieties, worries, and fears, and we ask for Your peace to reign in our hearts.

Still the storms within us, O Lord. Quiet the turbulence of our thoughts and emotions. Grant us a deep and abiding peace that can only come from You. Help us to cast our burdens upon You, trusting that You will sustain us and carry us through every challenge.

As we surrender to Your peace, teach us to be still and know that You are God. Guide us to find solace in Your presence, even in the midst of trials and uncertainties. Fill us with Your peace that transcends circumstances, anchoring us in the unshakable truth of Your love and faithfulness.

Lord, we also lift up to You those who are experiencing turmoil and unrest in their lives. Bring peace to their troubled hearts, O God. Comfort them with Your gentle touch and assure them of Your steadfast presence. Grant them the strength to navigate difficult situations and the wisdom to make choices that promote peace and harmony.

Prayer for Restoring Faith and Hope

Faithful God,

There are times when our faith wavers, when we struggle to trust in Your goodness and faithfulness. We confess that doubt and discouragement can sometimes cloud our vision and weaken our resolve. But we know that You are the God of restoration and hope.

Renew our faith, O Lord. Restore the confidence we have in Your promises. Help us to fix our eyes upon Jesus, the author and perfecter of our faith, knowing that in Him, we find hope that does not disappoint. Strengthen our belief in Your presence and Your power to bring about miracles and transformations.

In moments of doubt, Lord, remind us of Your faithfulness throughout history. Point us to the testimonies of Your goodness and grace in our own lives. Surround us with a community of believers who can uplift and encourage us in our faith journey.

Lord, we also pray for those who are wrestling with faith crises, who are questioning Your goodness and struggling to find hope. Reach out to them with Your tender love and compassion. Speak words of assurance and grace into their hearts. Show them that You are a God who delights in restoring faith and breathing new life into weary souls.

Help us, Lord, to be vessels of Your hope and encouragement. Give us the words to speak life and truth into the lives of others. Grant us the humility and compassion to walk alongside those who are struggling, offering them a listening ear, a comforting presence, and a word of hope.

As we seek the restoration of faith and hope, remind us that You are always at work, even in the midst of our doubts and questions. Help us to surrender our uncertainties to You and to trust in Your perfect timing and plan. Renew our hope in the promises of Your Word and the power of Your love.

May this chapter be a beacon of hope for those who are seeking spiritual healing. May it remind them that You are the God who restores, refreshes, and renews. May it inspire them to draw near to You, confident that in Your presence, they will find the healing and wholeness their souls desperately need.

In Your name, we pray for spiritual healing and well-being. Amen.

CHAPTER 5: PRAYERS FOR RELATIONAL HEALING

Prayer for Reconciliation in Relationships

Gracious God,

We come before You with heavy hearts, burdened by broken relationships and strained connections. We long for reconciliation and restoration, knowing that You are a God of reconciliation and peace. We acknowledge that healing broken relationships requires humility, forgiveness, and a willingness to bridge the gaps that divide us.

Lord, we lift up to You the relationships in our lives that are in need of reconciliation. Soften hearts that have grown hardened, and remove the barriers that hinder love and understanding. Grant us the courage to initiate conversations and extend forgiveness. Help us to see beyond our differences and to embrace the common ground we share as Your children.

In moments of conflict and discord, remind us of Your example of love and reconciliation. Teach us to love our enemies and to pray for those who have hurt us. Guide our words and actions, that they may be filled with grace, compassion, and understanding. Grant us the wisdom to discern when to speak and when to listen, when to confront and when to extend a hand of peace.

Lord, we also pray for those who are experiencing broken relationships. Bring healing and reconciliation to their lives, O God. Provide opportunities for open and honest communication. Heal wounds and restore trust. Help them to find the strength and courage to extend forgiveness and to seek reconciliation with those who have caused them pain.

May Your love and grace flow abundantly in our relationships, O Lord. May we be instruments of Your peace, agents of reconciliation, and bearers of Your love. May this chapter serve as a guide for praying earnestly and passionately for relational healing, knowing that Your power to mend what is broken exceeds our understanding.

Prayer for Forgiveness and Letting Go

Merciful Father,

We stand before You, aware of the weight of unforgiveness that burdens our souls. We acknowledge that holding on to resentment and bitterness only perpetuates pain and hinders our own growth and well-being. We come to You seeking the strength to forgive and the grace to let go.

Grant us, O Lord, the capacity to forgive as You have forgiven us. Help us to release the grip of anger, hurt, and disappointment. Teach us to see others through Your eyes, recognizing their brokenness and extending compassion. Fill our hearts with Your love, which covers a multitude of sins.

As we pray for the grace to forgive, we also pray for those who have wronged us. Soften their hearts, Lord, and grant them the gift of repentance. May they come to understand the pain they have caused and seek reconciliation. Help us to extend mercy and grace, even when it is difficult.

In the process of forgiveness, remind us that we are not condoning wrongdoing but choosing to free ourselves from the chains of resentment. Empower us to break the cycle of hurt and to build healthy boundaries in our relationships. Fill us with Your peace that surpasses understanding, knowing that true healing comes through forgiveness and letting go.

Prayer for Restoring Broken Bonds

Faithful God,

We come before You with hearts that long for the restoration of broken bonds. We lament the relationships that have been severed and the connections that have been damaged. We humbly ask for Your intervention and healing touch.

Lord, You are the God who restores and makes all things new. We pray for the restoration of broken bonds in our lives. Mend what has been torn apart, reconcile what has been divided, and heal what has been wounded. Bring unity and harmony where there is discord and strife.

We bring before You the broken bonds of families, friendships, marriages, and communities. Pour out Your love and grace, healing deep wounds and bridging the gaps that separate us. Help us to see the potential for reconciliation and restoration in every broken relationship. Give us the courage to initiate healing conversations, the humility to admit our faults, and the wisdom to seek understanding.

Lord, we also acknowledge that restoring broken bonds requires patience and perseverance. It may not happen overnight, and it may require ongoing efforts to rebuild trust and rebuild bridges. Grant us the endurance to stay committed to the process of reconciliation, even when it feels challenging or uncertain.

As we pray for the restoration of broken bonds, help us to cultivate an attitude of empathy and compassion. Open our hearts to truly listen to one another, to understand each other's perspectives, and to offer genuine apologies and forgiveness. Enable us to see the humanity in each other, recognizing that we are all imperfect and in need of grace.

Lord, we lift up to You those who are hurting from broken relationships. Comfort them in their pain and grant them the courage to seek reconciliation. Surround them with supportive and wise individuals who can guide them through the process of healing. Help them to find strength in You as they navigate the complexities of repairing broken bonds.

May this chapter be a source of hope and inspiration for those who long for restored relationships. May it serve as a reminder that with You, all things are possible, and that even the most broken relationships can experience redemption and healing.

In Your unfailing love and boundless grace, we trust and pray for the restoration of broken bonds. Amen.

CHAPTER 6: PRAYERS FOR HEALING IN TIMES OF LOSS

Prayer for Comfort in Grief and Loss

Heavenly Father,

In the midst of deep sorrow and loss, we turn to You, our source of comfort and strength. We bring before You the pain and anguish we feel, the tears that flow freely, and the emptiness that weighs heavy on our hearts. We seek Your comforting presence to soothe our souls and grant us the peace that surpasses all understanding.

Lord, You are near to the brokenhearted and bind up their wounds. Embrace us in Your loving arms and provide solace in this time of grief and loss. Help us to find comfort in Your promises, knowing that You are our refuge and our strength. Bring Your healing touch to our wounded hearts and restore our hope in the midst of despair.

Grant us the grace to mourn and grieve, for it is through the process of lament that healing begins. As we pour out our sorrows before You, enable us to find solace in Your presence and in the loving support of those around us. Surround us with compassionate friends and family who can offer a listening ear, a gentle word, and a comforting embrace.

Lord, we also lift up to You those who are experiencing grief and loss. Draw near to them, O God, and comfort them in their pain. Grant them the strength to navigate the difficult journey of mourning and the assurance that You are with them every step of the way. Bring healing to their broken hearts and fill their lives with renewed hope.

In the midst of sorrow, help us to cling to the hope we have in You. Remind us of the promise of eternal life and the assurance that one day, we will be reunited with our loved ones in Your heavenly presence. Until that day comes, grant us the strength to grieve, the courage to heal, and the peace that comes from knowing You are with us.

Prayer for Healing from the Pain of Bereavement

Compassionate God,

We come before You with heavy hearts, mourning the loss of loved ones who have departed from this earthly life. We feel the deep ache of their absence and the void they have left behind. We acknowledge the pain of bereavement and seek Your healing touch to mend our brokenness.

Lord, in the midst of our grief, help us to find solace in Your love and the assurance of eternal life. Remind us that those who have gone before us are now in Your presence, free from pain and suffering. Give us the strength to release them into Your loving care and to entrust them to Your faithful keeping.

As we navigate the path of bereavement, we ask for Your healing touch upon our wounded hearts. Bring comfort and peace to our souls as we mourn the loss of our loved ones. Help us to process our grief in healthy ways, allowing ourselves to feel the pain while also seeking support from others.

Grant us the grace to remember and honor the lives of those we have lost. May their memories be a source of inspiration and comfort, reminding us of the love and joy they brought into our lives. Help us to find healing in cherishing the precious moments we shared with them and carrying their legacies forward.

Lord, we also pray for others who are experiencing the pain of bereavement. Surround them with Your love and the support of a compassionate community. Give them the courage to lean on You and on others during this difficult season. Comfort them with Your presence and bring healing to their broken hearts.

In the midst of our pain, we hold on to the hope we have in You. We trust that You are a God who understands our grief and walks alongside us in our sorrow. Heal our hearts, O Lord, and grant us the strength to find joy.

Prayer for Strength and Hope in Times of Mourning

Gracious Father,

In the midst of our mourning and sorrow, we turn to You, the source of our strength and hope. We come before You with heavy hearts, seeking Your comforting presence to sustain us in this time of loss. We acknowledge our vulnerability and our need for

Your healing touch.

Lord, You are the God of all comfort, and You promise to be near to the brokenhearted. We ask for Your strength to endure the pain of loss and to navigate the journey of mourning. Fill us with Your peace that surpasses all understanding and grant us the courage to face each day with hope.

In times of grief, it is easy to feel overwhelmed and consumed by sadness. But we know that You are our refuge and our strength, a present help in times of trouble. Help us to find solace in Your presence and to draw strength from Your Word. Remind us of Your promises, that You will never leave us nor forsake us.

As we mourn the loss of our loved ones, we ask for Your healing touch upon our broken hearts. Bring comfort to our souls and grant us the strength to carry on. Help us to remember the legacy of love and joy that our departed loved ones have left behind. May their lives inspire us to live with purpose and to cherish the time we have with those still with us.

Lord, we also lift up to You those who are walking the journey of mourning. Surround them with Your loving arms and provide them with a community of support and understanding. Give them the strength to lean on others and to seek help when needed. Shower them with Your comfort and grant them moments of peace and healing.

In the midst of our grief, we choose to hold on to the hope we have in You. We trust that You will turn our mourning into dancing and our sorrow into joy. Help us to find meaning in the midst of loss and to embrace the gift of life that You have given us. Fill our hearts with gratitude for the time we shared with our loved ones and the memories we hold dear.

In Your unfailing love and tender mercy, we find our solace and our strength. We entrust our grief and our pain to You, knowing that You are faithful to bring healing and restoration. Grant us the strength to continue on this journey, walking hand in hand with You, until the day when all tears will be wiped away and joy will be restored.

We pray all these things in the name of Jesus, our Savior and Redeemer. Amen.

CHAPTER 7: PRAYERS FOR HEALING IN MARRIAGE AND FAMILY

Prayer for Restoring Love and Unity in Marriage

Heavenly Father,

We come before You with humble hearts, seeking Your divine intervention in our marriage. We acknowledge that there have been struggles and challenges that have strained the bond of love between us. We ask for Your healing touch to restore the love and unity that once defined our relationship.

Lord, You are the author of love and marriage, and You desire for us to experience the fullness of love and joy within the covenant of marriage. We confess that we have fallen short and allowed various factors to come between us. We ask for Your forgiveness for any words, actions, or attitudes that have hurt one another and damaged our relationship.

Father, we pray for a fresh outpouring of Your love and grace upon our hearts. Help us to see one another through Your eyes of compassion and understanding. Teach us to communicate with love and respect, seeking to build each other up rather than tearing each other down. Grant us the wisdom to prioritize our marriage and to invest the time and effort needed to nurture our relationship.

Lord, we surrender our marriage into Your hands. We trust that You can bring healing where there is brokenness, restoration where there is division, and unity where there is discord. Strengthen the bond of love between us and help us to cultivate a deep and lasting connection.

As we seek to restore our marriage, help us to let go of past hurts and to forgive one another as You have forgiven us. Fill our hearts with compassion and empathy, enabling us to extend grace and mercy to one another. May our words and actions reflect Your love and bring healing to the wounds within our relationship.

We invite Your Holy Spirit to dwell within our home,

guiding us in all aspects of our marriage. May Your presence bring peace, joy, and unity within our family. Help us to prioritize our commitment to one another and to create an environment of love and support for our children.

Lord, we pray for the strength and perseverance to overcome the challenges that come our way. Give us the wisdom to seek help when needed and to surround ourselves with a community of support and encouragement. Help us to grow together, deepening our love and commitment to one another with each passing day.

We thank You, Lord, for the gift of marriage and for the opportunity to grow and learn through the ups and downs of life together. We trust in Your faithfulness to bring healing and restoration to our relationship. May our marriage be a testament of Your love and grace to those around us.

We pray all these things in the name of Jesus, who is the foundation of our marriage. Amen.

Prayer for Healing and Reconciliation in Family

Loving Father,

We lift up our family before You, knowing that You desire for us to experience unity, love, and harmony within our midst. We acknowledge that there have been conflicts and divisions that have caused pain and brokenness in our family relationships. We come to You with open hearts, seeking Your healing touch and the power of Your reconciliation.

Lord, we ask for Your forgiveness for any words, actions, or attitudes that have caused hurt and division within our family. We pray for the humility to admit our own faults and the willingness to extend forgiveness to one another. Help us to let go of grudges and resentments, and fill our hearts with compassion and love for each other.

Father, we know that true healing and reconciliation can only come through You. We ask for Your Holy Spirit to work in the hearts of each family member, softening hardened hearts, and creating a spirit of forgiveness and understanding. Help us to see one another through Your eyes, valuing and cherishing the unique contributions each person brings to our family.

Lord, we pray for open and honest communication within our family. Give us the wisdom to express our thoughts and feelings in a respectful and loving manner. Help us to listen attentively to one another, seeking to understand rather than to respond defensively. Guide our conversations so that they may be filled with grace, compassion, and a genuine desire to reconcile and restore our relationships.

Heavenly Father, we ask for Your guidance in resolving conflicts and finding common ground. Grant us the wisdom to prioritize unity and harmony over personal agendas and desires. Help us to be quick to apologize and to seek forgiveness when we have wronged one another. Teach us to extend grace and mercy, just as You have shown us.

Lord, we pray for healing in the broken areas of our family relationships. Heal the wounds that have been caused by past hurts and misunderstandings. Restore trust where it has been broken and renew the love and affection we once shared. May Your love permeate every aspect of our family, bringing healing, peace, and reconciliation.

Father, we also recognize that healing and reconciliation may require effort and sacrifice from each family member. Give us the strength and commitment to actively work towards reconciliation, being willing to make amends, forgive, and let go of past grievances. Help us to create an environment of love, acceptance, and support within our family.

Lord, we surrender our family into Your hands. We trust in Your power to heal, restore, and reconcile. Fill our home with Your presence, Your peace, and Your joy. Help us to grow closer together as a family, strengthening the bonds that unite us.

We pray for Your continued guidance and wisdom as we navigate the challenges that may arise within our family. Give us the discernment to make decisions that honor You and promote unity and love. Help us to prioritize our relationships, investing time and effort in nurturing and strengthening the connections we share.

Lord, we thank You for the gift of family and for the opportunity to grow and learn through the challenges we face together. We trust in Your faithfulness to bring healing and reconciliation to our family. May our relationships be a reflection of Your love and grace, drawing others to experience the beauty of familial unity.

In Jesus' name, we pray. Amen.

Prayer for Blessings and Restoration in Parent-Child Relationships

Heavenly Father,

We come before You with grateful hearts, recognizing that You are the ultimate source of love and wisdom. We lift up our parent-child relationships to You, seeking Your blessings, guidance, and restoration in these precious connections.

Lord, we acknowledge that parenting is a sacred responsibility, and we confess that we have fallen short at times. We ask for Your forgiveness for any mistakes, shortcomings, or missed opportunities to nurture and guide our children. We pray for Your grace to cover our imperfections and to fill the gaps where we have fallen short.

Father, we pray for healing and restoration in our parent-child relationships. We ask for Your help in bridging any gaps that may exist between us and our children. Grant us the wisdom to understand their needs, desires, and aspirations. Help us to create an environment of trust, respect, and open communication where our children feel safe to express themselves and seek guidance.

Lord, we pray for reconciliation and forgiveness where there may be tension or estrangement in our parent-child relationships. Soften the hearts of both parents and children, granting us the humility to admit our mistakes, the willingness to forgive, and the courage to seek reconciliation. May Your love flow freely between us, restoring the bonds of love and affection.

Father, we also pray for Your blessings upon our children. Guide them in their growth and development, protecting them from harm and leading them on the path of righteousness. Help us, as parents, to be a source of encouragement, support, and guidance to our children. Give us the wisdom to understand their unique gifts, talents and passions, and help us to nurture and cultivate them in a way that brings them joy and fulfillment.

Lord, we ask for Your divine wisdom in parenting our children. Grant us the discernment to make decisions that align with Your will and that are in the best interest of our children's well-being and future. Help us to strike a balance between providing guidance and allowing them to grow and explore their own identities.

We pray for strength and patience as we navigate

the challenges of parenting. Grant us the resilience to weather the storms that may arise and the grace to extend understanding and forgiveness when mistakes are made. Help us to be consistent in our love and discipline, teaching our children valuable life lessons while also showing them unconditional love and acceptance.

Heavenly Father, we commit our parent-child relationships into Your loving care. We trust that You can bring healing, restoration, and blessings where they are needed. Help us to prioritize our relationships with our children, setting aside dedicated time to connect, communicate, and build memories together.

Lord, we also recognize that parenting is a journey of growth and learning. We ask for Your guidance and wisdom as we seek to become better parents each day. Surround us with a community of support and encouragement, providing mentors and resources that can help us in our parenting journey.

We thank You, Lord, for the precious gift of our children. We pray that our parent-child relationships may be a reflection of Your love, grace, and faithfulness. May our interactions with our children point them to You and nurture their own relationship with You. May our homes be filled with love, peace, and joy as we walk together on this beautiful journey of parenthood.

In Jesus' name, we pray. Amen.

CHAPTER 8: PRAYERS FOR INNER STRENGTH AND EMPOWERMENT

Prayer for Courage and Confidence

Heavenly Father, I come before You seeking courage and confidence in the face of challenges and uncertainties. You are the source of all strength, and I ask that You fill me with Your divine power and boldness. Help me to trust in Your promises and believe in Your plans for my life. Grant me the courage to step out of my comfort zone, to face my fears, and to pursue the dreams and goals You have placed in my heart. May Your Spirit guide me and empower me to walk in faith, knowing that You are with me every step of the way. In Jesus' name, I pray. Amen.

Prayer for Overcoming Challenges and Obstacles

Gracious God, I lift up to You the challenges and obstacles that stand in my way. I acknowledge that on my own, I am weak and limited, but with You, all things are possible. Grant me the strength and perseverance to overcome every hurdle that comes my way. Help me to view challenges as opportunities for growth and refinement. Fill me with Your wisdom and creativity to find innovative solutions and strategies. Lord, I place my trust in You, knowing that You are my refuge and strength in times of trouble. I am confident that as I rely on You, I will emerge victorious, strengthened, and equipped to fulfill Your purpose for my life. In Jesus' name, I believe and pray. Amen.

Prayer for Empowerment and Steadfastness

Mighty God, I humbly come before You, seeking Your empowerment and steadfastness in my journey. I acknowledge that apart from You, I can do nothing of lasting value. I surrender my plans, desires, and ambitions into Your hands. Fill me with Your Holy Spirit and equip me with the gifts and talents needed to fulfill Your purposes. Strengthen my inner being, that I may stand firm in the face of trials and opposition. Help me to stay rooted in Your Word and to rely on Your promises. Grant me the grace to persevere, even when the path is difficult and the way seems long. I trust that You will provide me with the endurance and resilience needed to run this race with faith and endurance. In the name of Jesus, I pray. Amen.

CHAPTER 9: PRAYERS FOR OVERALL WELL-BEING

Prayer for a Healthy Mind, Body, and Spirit

Heavenly Father, I come before You with a humble heart, seeking Your divine touch upon my mind, body, and spirit. You are the Creator of all things, and I acknowledge that my well-being is in Your hands. I pray for the restoration and preservation of my health. Grant me physical strength, vitality, and endurance to carry out the tasks set before me. Heal any sickness or disease that may be present in my body. Renew my mind, filling it with clarity, wisdom, and peace. Nourish my spirit, that I may experience a deep and abiding connection with You. Help me to steward my health well, making choices that honor and glorify You. May my entire being be a reflection of Your goodness and grace. In Jesus' name, I pray.

Amen.

Prayer for Emotional Balance and Stability

Loving Father, I lift up to You my emotions, knowing that You understand and care for the depths of my heart. I ask for Your grace and guidance in achieving emotional balance and stability. Help me to navigate through the ups and downs of life with wisdom and grace. Grant me the strength to overcome negative emotions such as anxiety, fear, and sadness. Fill me with Your peace that surpasses all understanding. Help me to cultivate healthy coping mechanisms and to seek support when needed. May Your Spirit work in me, transforming my emotional well-being, so that I may experience joy, peace, and resilience even in the midst of trials. In Jesus' name, I pray. Amen.

Prayer for Gratitude and Contentment

Heavenly Father, I come before You with a heart filled with gratitude for the blessings You have bestowed upon me. I thank You for the gift of life, for Your provision, and for the love and relationships in my life. Help me to cultivate an attitude of gratitude in all circumstances, knowing that You are working all things together for my good. Guard my heart against discontentment and comparison. Teach me to find contentment in Your presence and in the knowledge of Your unfailing love. Fill me with a spirit of generosity and compassion, that I may bless others and share the abundance You have given me. May my life be a testimony of gratitude and contentment, shining Your light into the world. In Jesus' name, I pray. Amen.

CONCLUSION

In this book, "Prayers for Healing and Well-being: Finding Comfort, Renewing Strength, and Experiencing Wholeness," we have explored various aspects of healing and well-being, addressing physical, emotional, mental, spiritual, and relational needs. Through the power of prayer, we have sought solace, restoration, and renewal in every area of our lives.

Throughout these chapters, we have discovered that healing is not just about the mending of our bodies or the restoration of our circumstances; it is a holistic process that involves our entire being. We have learned to surrender our burdens to God, trusting in His love and faithfulness to bring healing and restoration.

It is important to remember that healing is not always immediate or in the form we expect. God works in His perfect timing and His ways are higher than our own. Through prayer, we have found strength, comfort, and hope in the midst of our trials. We have experienced the peace that surpasses all understanding, and we have witnessed the transformative power of God's love in our lives.

As we conclude this journey of prayer and healing, let us continue to seek God's presence and guidance in our lives. May we remain steadfast in our faith, trusting that He is always working for our good. Let us embrace the process of healing, knowing that it is through our brokenness that God's light can shine brightest.

I encourage you to make these prayers a part of your daily life, not just in times of need, but as a continuous practice of seeking God's presence and experiencing His healing touch. May these prayers serve as a source of comfort, strength, and inspiration as you walk the path of healing and well-being.

May you find comfort in knowing that you are never alone on this journey. God is with you every step of the way, and He longs to bring healing and wholeness to every aspect of your life. Open your heart to His love, receive His healing touch, and embrace the abundant life He has prepared for you.

May these prayers be a source of encouragement and a reminder that you are deeply loved and cherished by your Creator. May you experience the fullness of His healing and well-being, finding comfort, renewing strength, and experiencing wholeness in every area of your life.

May God's blessings be upon you as you journey on the path of healing and well-being.

Final Prayer of Blessing

Heavenly Father, we thank You for guiding us through this book of prayers for healing and well-being. We lift up every reader to Your loving care. Pour out Your blessings upon them, granting them comfort, strength, and renewal. May Your healing touch bring wholeness to their bodies, minds, and spirits. Fill their hearts with Your peace and surround them with Your love.

As they continue to seek You in prayer, may they experience the power of Your presence and the transformation that comes through Your grace. Equip them to walk in faith, trusting in Your goodness and faithfulness. Help them to embrace the journey of healing and well-being, knowing that You are with them every step of the way.

May Your light shine through their lives, drawing others to Your healing love. Use them as vessels of Your compassion and grace, bringing hope and restoration to those around them. May their testimonies be a testament to Your faithfulness and the power of prayer.

We commit each reader into Your hands, knowing that You are the ultimate healer and provider of all good things. May they find comfort, renew their strength, and experience the fullness of Your love as they seek Your face in prayer.

In Jesus' name, we pray. Amen.

Milton Keynes UK
Ingram Content Group UK Ltd.
UKHW020326031224
451863UK00012B/419